Refocus and Recharge!

50 Brain Breaks for Middle Schoolers

Responsive Classroom®

All net proceeds from the sale of this book support the work of Center for Responsive Schools, Inc., a not-for-profit educational organization and the developer of the *Responsive Classroom*® approach to teaching.

The stories in this book are all based on real events. However, in order to respect individuals' privacy, names and many identifying characteristics have been changed.

ISBN: 978-1-892989-87-1
Library of Congress Control Number: 2016907103

Photographs by Jeff Woodward
Handout images by Jim Brissette, Laura Heisig, and Sera Rivers

Center for Responsive Schools wishes to thank the many people whose hard work and dedication to students and educators have made this book possible. Special thanks go to middle school educators Joe Tilley and Andy Moral for their careful reading of and feedback on the manuscript.

Center for Responsive Schools, Inc.
85 Avenue A, P.O. Box 718
Turners Falls, MA 01376-0718

800-360-6332
www.responsiveclassroom.org

Fourth printing 2020

Contents

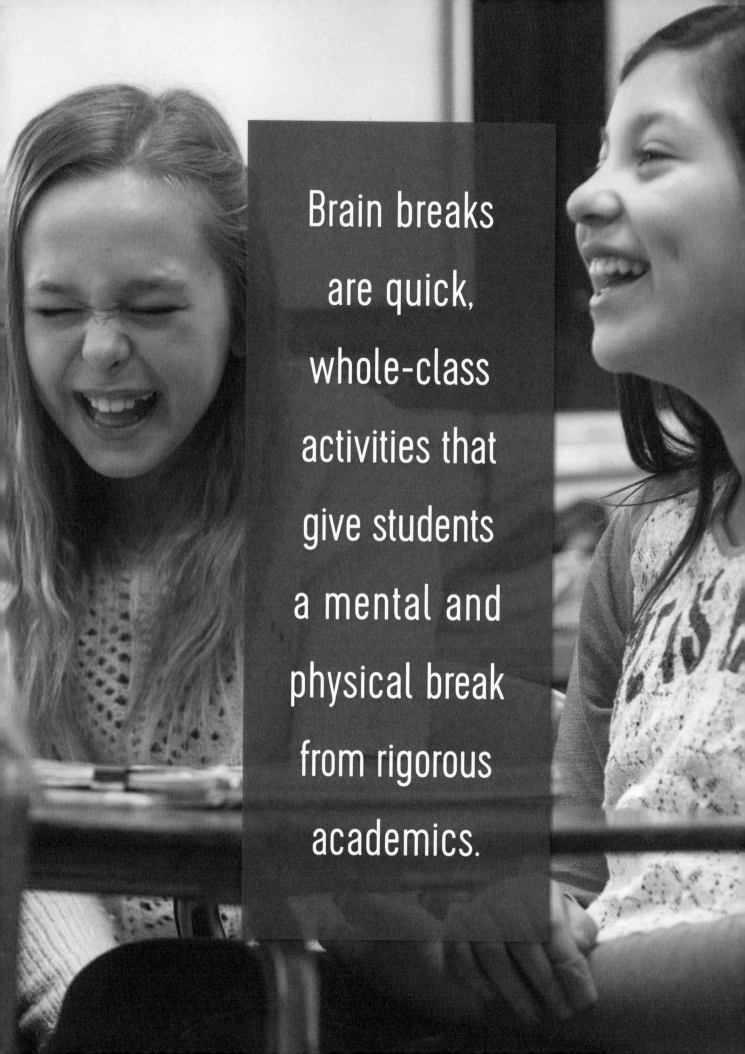

Brain breaks are quick, whole-class activities that give students a mental and physical break from rigorous academics.

Getting Started With Brain Breaks

What Are Brain Breaks?

Brain breaks are quick, whole-class activities that give students a mental and physical break from rigorous academics. Students can stand up, stretch, and move. They might listen to a brief calming or inspiring reading, visualize a peaceful image, or try to beat the class record for doing a mental or physical task. Whether calming or energetic, brain breaks:

➤ Refresh the brain and body so students feel alert

➤ Give students a safe and structured way to connect with peers and teachers

➤ Refocus students' attention so they're ready for more—and more productive—learning

Because brain breaks are so versatile and easy to do, you can use them at any point in the school day and at any time during a class period. For example, you might use a calming one like Solar Power (p. 56) or Soothing Sounds (p. 57) when students' energies are high, such as after lunch or PE. And you might use an energetic one like Body Drumming (p. 18) or Fidget Family (p. 24) when students' energies are low, such as after a big test or an especially challenging assignment.

Why Are Brain Breaks So Powerful?

Middle schoolers are at an age when they need frequent opportunities to pause, move, and interact to recharge themselves and refocus their energies. By responding to these developmental needs, brain breaks promote the academic and social growth of young adolescents. And by giving teachers efficient ways to help students stay focused on and enthusiastic about learning, brain breaks also support strong teaching.

Helping Adolescents Grow

Adolescence is a time of rapid change and growth. Bodies mature and brains undergo a complex reorganization. Moral and ethical reasoning abilities increase, as does awareness of and respect for other people's points of view, feelings, and rights. At the same time, the flood of hormones that intensifies adolescents' moods and everyday experiences can make it hard for them to control impulses and make good decisions.

Because of this intense development, middle schoolers need frequent opportunities to recharge their energies so they can continue functioning at high levels academically and socially. Brain breaks are convenient, structured ways to give students these opportunities while also promoting their further growth in three key areas:

➤ **Social-emotional development**—Social-emotional skills are the essential underpinnings of academic growth. This is especially crucial for young adolescents, who have a strong interest in being with and learning from their peers. Brain breaks help students develop the social-emotional skills they need to master rigorous academics in the intensely social context of middle school.

➤ **Cognitive development**—Every brain break includes movement, which sends the brain oxygen, water, and glucose. These vital substances help the brain grow and improve students' mood, memory, and motivation, all of which are essential to learning. Movement also stimulates brain cells to bind together in ways that further support learning. And brain breaks help students build their critical thinking skills as they form mental pictures, make quick decisions, and follow motion or word patterns.

➤ **Physical development**—Movement can help release excess energy and ease physical tension. By combining safe movement with purposeful social interactions, brain breaks offer a quick and convenient way to support students during this time of rapid development.

Boosting Academic and Social Skills

The benefits of brain breaks tend to carry over to other aspects of students' school lives. Students take positive risks as they learn and practice brain breaks, so you'll likely see them gradually take more academic risks, too. Brain breaks also have a strong classroom community component, which helps students build the skills needed for positive relationships with their peers and teachers.

Here's a summary of the skills brain breaks help students develop:

ACADEMIC SKILLS

- **Academic mindset**—Many brain breaks give students opportunities to improve their cognitive abilities as they do successive rounds or come up with ways to vary an activity. These fun opportunities to surpass personal achievements through practice help nurture the belief that abilities are not fixed but rather grow with effort.

- **Academic perseverance**—Brain breaks inherently require students to persevere, whether in guessing answers from classmates' clues, coming up with new ideas to act out, or keeping their eyes closed and minds focused as they create a mental image of a peaceful scene. These enjoyable experiences with perseverance help build students' ability to persist in working hard when facing academic challenges.

SOCIAL-EMOTIONAL SKILLS

- **Cooperation**—Brain breaks give students opportunities to practice cooperation as they work together in meeting a common objective.

- **Assertiveness**—Students learn to positively assert themselves when they share ideas during a brain break, suggest ways the class can improve its speed or dexterity, or volunteer to lead an activity.

- **Responsibility**—Brain breaks teach students to take responsibility when they actively participate, both as individuals and as group members.

- **Empathy**—Students learn to be understanding and helpful when a classmate gets confused or makes a mistake; they see that brain breaks are the most fun when everyone feels included and valued.

- **Self-control**—All brain breaks require self-control as students regulate their thoughts, emotions, and behavior for everyone's safety and enjoyment.

Strengthening Teaching Effectiveness

Whether you teach students for short periods or longer blocks, brain breaks will strengthen your effectiveness by helping you maintain a productive and positive learning environment through:

- **Effective classroom management**—Brain breaks can be a key tool in managing the classroom because they engage wandering minds and reduce off-task behaviors. Providing just enough of a break to help students recharge and refocus enables everyone to make the most of limited class time.

➤ **A positive classroom community**—Besides craving opportunities to social-
ize, middle schoolers show a heightened sensitivity to classmates' opinions and
ideas. Brain breaks help you build and maintain a positive classroom community by enabling safe, productive peer-to-peer interactions. Brain breaks also
motivate students to do their best by requiring individual and group effort and
giving them opportunities to develop leadership and teamwork skills.

Getting the Most Out of Brain Breaks

The following tips will help you choose among the 50 brain breaks in this book and
use them in ways that provide maximum benefits for students.

Choose and Adapt Brain Breaks to Fit Student Needs

Let your knowledge of students guide your choices. Ask yourself:

➤ **Where are students developmentally?** Students are most likely to succeed
when you choose brain breaks that match their developmental needs. For example, at the beginning of the year, you might choose Just Like Me! (p. 34) as a low-
risk way to introduce brain breaks and help build positive relationships. Once
students are more familiar with one another and more capable of taking academic and social-emotional risks, you might try a more challenging one, such
as Three-Person Machine (p. 59).

➤ **What are students' energy levels?** Group and individual energy levels go up
and down throughout the day and vary depending on group dynamics. For example, you might use Imagine This (p. 31) to calm one group of students coming in
from PE and Shake It Down (p. 51) to revitalize another group during the last
period of the day.

➤ **How can I maximize classroom space?** You can adapt any brain break to suit
the shape and size of your particular classroom. If the activity calls for students
to stand in a circle but you lack adequate space, you can easily change the format
to have students form several small circles, stand in two facing lines, or remain at
their desks.

➤ **What are we studying?** Although brain breaks are designed to give students
a mental break from academic content, you can connect any of them to learning in an informal way. With Picture This (p. 48), for example, you could have
students imagine a geographic location, cultural setting, or time period that
ties in to a current unit of study.

Use Positive Teacher Language

Using positive language as you guide students through brain breaks will help them enjoy and benefit from each one. By keeping your words, tone, and pace light and encouraging, you signal to students that you want them to have fun together while still being mindful of behavior expectations. Here are some examples of positive teacher language that you can use to ensure students' success with brain breaks:

> **Reinforcing language**—Identifying and affirming what students are doing well encourages them to repeat and build on successful behaviors: "You all moved around the room silently and slowly as you looked for the other half of your quote. That helped everyone concentrate on finding their match."

> **Reminding language**—Reminders prompt students to remember for themselves the expectations you've taught: "Who can remind us what to do if your partner gets stuck on thinking up the pros or cons of a topic?"

> **Open-ended questions**—These questions, which have no right or wrong answer, draw on middle schoolers' thoughts, knowledge, skills, experiences, and feelings: "What are some strategies you might use to keep your balance as you do the actions for Twisted Brain?"

To go deeper with positive teacher language, check out *Power of Our Words for Middle School: Teacher Language That Helps Students Learn* from *Responsive Classroom*® (2016) or visit www.responsiveclassroom.org for additional resources.

Emphasize Quality Over Quantity

You and your students will likely enjoy experimenting with many of the brain breaks in this book, but don't worry if you find yourself returning to a trusted few. Middle schoolers often enjoy the sense of community that comes from doing "their" brain breaks. If you sense that students would benefit from some variety, mix in a new one every now and then.

Decide in Advance Who Does What

Many brain breaks involve simple tasks, such as leading the class through the actions, reading aloud, or turning music on and off. It's best to handle these tasks yourself the first few times you do a brain break. Once everyone's familiar with the activity, you might ask for student volunteers. Over time, try to make sure everyone who wants to help out gets a chance to do so.

Try Using a Timing Tool

Using a timing tool can help students pace themselves to keep the brain break moving along. Timing the activity can also keep things fresh by adding an additional challenge as students try to beat their previous completion time for energetic breaks like Number Freeze (p. 43) and Zoom (p. 66). Any timer is fine, whether a digital timer you project on the wall or whiteboard or an auditory signal like a bell, music clip, or chime. You can serve as timekeeper yourself or assign the role to a student.

State the Expectations

It's important to emphasize that you expect everyone to participate and that both individual and group effort determine success. Remind students of these expectations whenever they're about to begin a brain break, especially ones that involve partners or small groups like Double This, Double That (p. 20) and Group Charades (p. 27).

Students who need time to build a level of comfort before actively participating can turn lights or music off and on, keep time, take photos of the group, or make quick sketches to share with the class. After you use the same brain break a few times, they'll likely feel ready and eager to join in.

Model and Practice Each Brain Break

Brain breaks work best when students fully grasp the actions involved and the type of behavior expected, so it's important to teach each activity before using it. The simple, four-step procedure of Interactive Modeling is an effective way to do this teaching. You'll find that the few extra minutes you take to model and practice with students will improve their ability to focus and maintain positive behavior while also having fun.

Here's how Interactive Modeling might look and sound if you used it to teach Encore Brainwriting (p. 23).

Interactive Modeling Steps	What It Might Sound/Look Like
1 **Describe what you will model and why.** Your brief statement helps students focus.	"Time for Encore Brainwriting! You'll have one minute on your own to brainstorm and list songs that have the word 'energy' in the title or lyrics. When I ring the chime, your group will sort out which songs are unique and which are repeats, and you'll note personal connections you have with the songs. Your group's recorder will summarize the results."
2 **Model while students watch.** Don't narrate as you demonstrate; instead, let students concentrate on observing the key aspects for themselves. As needed, prepare student volunteers in advance to assist you. After modeling, ask students what they noticed.	"Watch as Justin, Rakesh, and I brainwrite and then sort out the songs. Justin will be the recorder. . . . What did you notice about what we did?" Possible student responses: ➤ "Everyone wrote neatly so Justin could read the lists of songs." ➤ "You and Rakesh stayed quiet when you finished because time wasn't up and Justin was still writing." ➤ "Everyone shared ideas about connections they had to the songs."
3 **Give students the opportunity to practice.** This helps students get the steps down while your demonstration is fresh in their minds.	"Now let's practice Encore Brainwriting as a class. Form groups of three with your immediate neighbors. I'll watch you all brainwrite just the way you saw us demonstrate."
4 **Reinforce students' practice with immediate feedback.** Name specific, positive actions and respectfully correct mistakes to solidify students' understanding.	➤ "I saw many of you taking time to think before writing down songs." ➤ "I noticed many of you actively listening while waiting for a turn to speak."

Liven It Up or Slow It Down

Some of the brain breaks in this book begin energetically and end peacefully. For example, take a look at Do What I Said, Not What I Say (p. 21) and Let It Rain (p. 35). Others, such as Ma Zinga (p. 37) and Password (p. 44), do just the opposite.

And you can easily adapt any brain break to be more lively or calming by:

➤ Changing the movements

➤ Doing the actions silently or adjusting the volume

➤ Choosing music with a faster or slower beat

➤ Eliminating or adding a chant or song

➤ Ending with an enthusiastic cheer or a few calming breaths

It's Time for a Brain Break

The best way to start using brain breaks is to dive right in. Check the list that follows to choose a brain break by type—refocusing or recharging. Then scan the "In Brief" column to find one you think students will enjoy.

Once you choose a brain break, turn to its page and you'll find what you need to teach it quickly and efficiently:

➤ Clear, simple instructions

➤ Sample actions and words

➤ Tips for success

➤ Suggested variations

With just a small investment of time up front to choose and integrate brain breaks into your classroom routines, you'll see how these quick, easy activities help increase student alertness and productivity. The more you use brain breaks purposefully, the more opportunities you'll have to refocus and recharge students—and yourself!

Choose a Brain Break

TITLE	REFOCUS	RECHARGE	IN BRIEF	PAGE
Air Writing	●●● ●●● ●●●		Write in the air to slow down and focus on the present moment.	14
Alive Times Five!		●●● ●○● ●●●	Do a simple chant and invigorating movements.	15
And Don't You Forget It!		●●● ●○● ●●●	Recall information and listen closely with this speedy memory game.	16
Beach Ball Toss		●●● ●○● ●●●	Toss a beach ball for a low-key way to move—and practice academic skills.	17
Body Drumming		●●● ●○● ●●●	Create the sound of a drum orchestra by rhythmically stomping and clapping.	18
Calming Moments	●●● ●●● ●●●		Ease tension and relax with deep breathing and gentle motions.	19
Double This, Double That		●●● ●○● ●●●	Do this upbeat hand-tapping sequence with partners to refresh classroom spirits.	20
Do What I Said, Not What I Say		●●● ●○● ●●●	Stay one action behind the leader for a stimulating version of Simon Says.	21
Elevens		●●● ●○● ●●●	Try to total eleven in a fast-paced game of chance.	22
Encore Brainwriting		●●● ●○● ●●●	Brainstorm song titles; then sort them with a group and make personal connections.	23
Fidget Family		●●● ●○● ●●●	Get rejuvenated through lively actions with this quirky, read-aloud story.	24
The Four Elements	●●● ●●● ●●●		Quiet body and mind with peaceful words and motions.	26

	Choose a Brain Break				
TITLE	**REFOCUS**	**RECHARGE**	**IN BRIEF**	**PAGE**
Group Charades		●●●●●●●	Incorporate vocabulary practice into a classic guessing game.	27
Hands Up!		●●●●●●●	Quickly recall information while clapping and chanting.	28
Have a Ball		●●●●●●●	Mimic how the leader tosses and catches a paper ball.	29
Humdingers		●●●●●●●	Hum one of four songs while seeking others who are humming the same song.	30
Imagine This	●●●●●●●●●		Build a detailed mental image through guided meditation.	31
Interruptions	●●●●●●●●●		Unwind by making punctuation sounds as a poem or passage is read aloud.	32
In the Bag	●●●●●●●●●		Visualize "balling up" excess energy or worry and "throwing it away."	33
Just Like Me!		●●●●●●●	Make personal connections by seeing who responds to the leader's statements.	34
Let It Rain	●●●●●●		Imitate storm sounds—high energy of thunder, calmness of rain.	35
Love It or Leave It		●●●●●●●	Learn about each other as everyone practices "on the spot" decision-making.	36
Ma Zinga		●●●●●●●	Build up and then release energy with a team cheer!	37
Mellow Echo	●●●●●●		Follow simple motions to focus on the present moment.	38
Metaphorical Connections	●●●●●●●●●		Make creative connections between everyday objects and academic content.	39

Brain Breaks at a Glance

⠿ Refocus

⠿ Recharge

Air Writing

In Brief

Write in the air to slow down and focus on the present moment.

Skills Practiced

Building vocabulary

Concentration

Coordination

Recalling/retaining information

Time Frame

1–2 minutes

Materials

None

Variations

For a challenge, write with the nondominant hand or with elbow, shoulder, knee, foot, or nose.

Pair up. Partners take turns choosing a vocabulary word to air write. The observer tries to guess the word.

How to Do It

1 **The leader calls out a familiar word** from a list of vocabulary words or key terms.

2 **Students thoughtfully and slowly write** the word in the air with the pointer finger of their dominant hand.

Tips for Success

➤ Make sure students sit or stand in a comfortable position. Have them take a few slow, deep breaths before starting to help them relax.

➤ Encourage students to visualize each letter as they air write, make a mental image of the completed word, and then reflect on its meaning.

Alive Times Five!

In Brief

Do a simple chant and invigorating movements.

Skills Practiced

Concentration
Coordination
Self-awareness

Time Frame

1–2 minutes

Materials

None

Variation

Once students know this brain break well, they can say the chant silently to themselves and do the actions as quietly as possible.

How to Do It

1 **Students stand at their desks** or in a circle.

2 **Everyone chants** while performing the actions in unison:

"I am . . ."

"Awake!" (stretch arms out wide)

"Alert!!" (snap fingers)

"Alive!!!" (clap hands twice)

Repeat five times.

3 **End with everyone exclaiming "Alive times five!"** and doing an energetic movement chosen beforehand, such as a few jumping jacks.

Tip for Success

➤ Start slowly and speed up as students become more familiar with the actions.

B R A I N   B I T
Positive thoughts can help the brain process information and emotions more effectively.

And Don't You Forget It!

In Brief

Recall information and listen closely with this speedy memory game.

Skills Practiced

Active listening

Clear speaking

Concentration

Recalling/retaining information

Time Frame

3–4 minutes

Materials

None

Variations

For a shorter version, students say just their own statement; then, in unison, the whole class says, "And don't you forget it!"

For added challenge, make a "no repeats" rule.

How to Do It

1 **Students stand** at their desks or in a circle.

2 **Choose a topic** (academic or personal). For example: "Things to remember about persuasive essays." Give students a moment to think of their response (a phrase or word related to the topic).

3 **The first student looks at the next person** and says, "I say 'thesis statement,' and don't you forget it!"

4 **The second student looks at the next person** and says, "Joaquin said 'thesis statement,' I say 'research,' and don't you forget it!"

5 **The third student looks at the next person** and says, "Min said 'research,' I say 'detailed paragraphs,' and don't you forget it!" Continue around the room until everyone has had a turn or time is up (you can continue next class period).

Tips for Success

➤ Teach students what to do if they go off topic or forget. This activity is meant to move quickly, so you could give students the option to say "Pass."

➤ For personal topics, discuss with students what's appropriate to share.

Beach Ball Toss

In Brief

Toss a beach ball for a low-key way to move—and practice academic skills.

Skills Practiced

Coordination

Mental math

Recalling/retaining information

Time Frame

2–3 minutes

Materials

Beach ball

Dry-erase marker

Optional: Paper strips

Variation

Instead of numbers, use key terms, historical events, or literary characters, and have students explain how the two (closest to their hands) are related.

How to Do It

These directions give a math example, but you can adapt this brain break for any subject area.

1 **Beforehand, write a number** on each panel of a beach ball and on the small circles at the top and bottom. (Or write on strips of paper and tape them to the ball.)

2 **Students stand at their desks or in a circle.** Announce what students will do—for example, add integers—and then toss the ball to a student.

3 **The person who catches the ball** chooses two numbers closest to their hands and solves the equation. For example: The student mentally adds +3 (left hand) and –10 (right hand), then says, "Positive three plus negative ten equals negative seven."

4 **The student tosses the ball to someone else,** and the activity continues until everyone has had a turn or time is up (you can continue next class period). With each toss, you or the student tossing the ball can change the operation to subtraction, multiplication, or division.

Tip for Success

➤ Go over the mental math steps and discuss what to do if a student answers incorrectly. For example, you might pause the activity by saying, "Let's double check that," and then as a class go through the steps to find the correct answer.

Body Drumming

In Brief

Create the sound of a drum orchestra by rhythmically stomping and clapping.

Skills Practiced

Concentration

Coordination

Differentiating

Teamwork

Time Frame

1–2 minutes

Materials

None

Variation

For a challenge, create more elaborate body drumming patterns.

How to Do It

1 **Students stand and spread out** so they have enough room to do the motions safely.

2 **Teach and practice a three-count stomp-and-clap pattern:**
   Stomp . . . stomp . . . clap
   Stomp . . . stomp . . . clap

3 **Teach and practice a four-count pattern:**
   Stomp . . . stomp . . . stomp . . . clap
   Stomp . . . stomp . . . stomp . . . clap

4 **Divide the class in half and combine the stomps:** Half the class does the three-count pattern; the other half does the four-count pattern. On your signal, everyone starts at the same time.

5 **After 1–2 minutes,** signal for all students to stop at the same time.

Tips for Success

➤ If needed, model and practice how to stay in one's own personal space. (See p. 7 for Interactive Modeling steps.)

➤ Start off slowly and speed up as students become more familiar with the moves.

BRAIN BIT
When students find school engaging, they're more likely to retain what they learn.

Calming Moments

In Brief

Ease tension and relax with deep breathing and gentle motions.

Skills Practiced

Active listening

Concentration

Deep breathing

Self-awareness

Time Frame

1–3 minutes

Materials

None

Variation

For an energizer, change calming motions to clapping ones (clap, rest, clap, clap, rest) and eliminate the deep breathing. Optional: Make up a chant or song to perform while doing the motions.

How to Do It

1 **Students sit in a circle** or at their desks as the leader guides them through calming motions and breathing exercises, such as:

"Inhale deeply through your nose for a count of three, then pause . . ." (raise arms toward the ceiling)

"Slowly exhale through your mouth for a count of four . . ." (slowly lower arms to sides)

2 **The leader repeats the words and motions** several times and then changes the pattern. For example:

"Inhale deeply for a count of four, then pause . . ." (extend arms in front of body parallel to ground with hands closed; pull arms straight back until hands reach sides)

"Now slowly exhale for a count of five . . ." (open hands, raise them so palms face outward; slowly push hands away from body)

3 **To conclude,** the leader stops the motions, takes three short breaths through the nose, and exhales one long breath through the mouth. Students echo this breathing and finish with a few seconds of silence.

Tip for Success

➤ Before starting, brainstorm different motions and breathing patterns the class can try.

Double This, Double That

In Brief

Do this upbeat hand-tapping sequence with partners to refresh classroom spirits.

Skills Practiced

Concentration

Coordination

Teamwork

Time Frame

1–2 minutes

Materials

None

Variations

Form two circles, one inside the other, with students facing each other. Switch partners after each round by having the outside circle move one person to the right.

For a challenge, chant and tap faster each round.

For a calming activity, do the last two rounds silently or in a whisper.

How to Do It

1 **Students stand facing a partner** with arms in front of them and bent at the elbow; hands are loosely closed at about chest level.

2 **In unison, partners do a series of hand motions** while they chant, as follows:

"Double Double"	(tap pinkie side of fists twice against pinkie side of partner's fists)
"This This!"	(tap palms twice against partner's palms)
"Double Double"	(tap pinkie side of fists twice against pinkie side of partner's fists)
"That That!"	(tap back of hands twice against back of partner's hands)
"Double This!"	(tap fists once against partner's fists and then tap palms once against partner's palms)
"Double That!"	(tap fists once against partner's fists and then tap back of hands once against back of partner's hands)
"Double Double"	(tap pinkie side of fists twice against pinkie side of partner's fists)
"This That!"	(tap palms once against partner's palms and then tap back of hands once against back of partner's hands)

Tip for Success

➤ Emphasize that all motions need to be gentle.

Do What I Said, Not What I Say

In Brief

Stay one action behind the leader for a stimulating version of Simon Says.

Skills Practiced

Active listening

Concentration

Coordination

Differentiating

Time Frame

1–3 minutes

Materials

None

Variation

To add greater challenge, the leader may also do the action while calling it out.

How to Do It

1 **Everyone stands at their desks** or in a circle. The leader calls out an action.

2 **Students must follow the previously given action,** not the current one. Here's a sample set of leader instructions and student responses:

"Stand on one foot!"	(students do nothing)
"Hop on one foot!"	(students stand on one foot)
"Flap your arms!"	(students hop on one foot)
"Pat your head!"	(students flap their arms)
"Sit down!"	(students pat their heads)
"Fold your hands on your desks!"	(students sit down)
"Fold your hands on your desks!"	(students fold their hands on their desks and are ready for the next lesson or activity)

Tip for Success

➤ Make sure students have enough room to perform all actions safely.

Elevens

In Brief

Try to total eleven in a fast-paced game of chance.

Skills Practiced

Concentration

Mental math

Teamwork

Time Frame

2–4 minutes

Materials

None

Variation

Instead of forming new groups at Step 4, keep the original groups but give a new target number.

How to Do It

1 **Students form circles** of four or five and stand with one hand behind their backs.

2 **Each group says in unison** "One, two, three—eleven!" On "eleven," group members "throw" one hand into the center of the circle as they flash any number of fingers—from zero (a fist) to five—to try to total eleven fingers.

3 **If the number of fingers does not equal eleven,** group members try again.

4 **If the number of fingers equals eleven,** the group does a brief, celebratory cheer (decided in advance). Then the group joins another group and continues playing with them.

5 **If all groups merge into one** (whole class) within the allotted time, form new groups and play again.

Tips for Success

➤ Tell students they cannot do any verbal group strategizing or give clues as to what number they might "throw."

➤ Brainstorm a cheer (for example, saying "Yes!" and pumping a fist in the air).

B R A I N   B I T
Brain breaks can help strengthen higher-order thinking by providing opportunities for synthesizing information, making quick decisions, and solving problems.

Encore Brainwriting

In Brief

Brainstorm song titles; then sort them with a group and make personal connections.

Skills Practiced

Brainstorming

Categorizing

Making personal connections

Teamwork

Time Frame

3–5 minutes

Materials

Small sticky notes

T-chart handouts (see p. 69) or large sheets of paper

Pencils or pens

Variations

Instead of calling out words in Step 2, hold up a photo (such as one from pp. 89–95).

Instead of songs, brainstorm related books, poems, historical figures, events, or places.

How to Do It

1 **Students form groups** of three or four. Give each group sticky notes and the T-chart handout (see p. 69) or a large sheet of paper; assign a recorder, or let students choose their own.

2 **Call out a vocabulary word, theme, or category** (for example: independence). Explain that the goal is to think of as many songs as possible that have that word in the title or lyrics. The recorder makes a T-chart (or uses the handout) and writes the word in the left-hand column.

3 **Signal students to begin.** Give them one minute to write down their songs (one title or lyric per sticky note). Students post their sticky notes under the word on their group's T-chart.

4 **As a group, students identify** which songs are repeats and which are unique. They also share any connections to the songs (for example, everyone in the group has sung it at a party).

5 **The recorder uses the right-hand column** of the T-chart to summarize the results. Then the group displays their finished chart.

Tips for Success

➤ Explain that brainwriting is a type of brainstorming where you write down your thoughts before sharing them aloud with your group.

➤ Discuss what types of songs and lyrics are appropriate for sharing.

Fidget Family

In Brief

Get rejuvenated through lively actions with this quirky, read-aloud story.

Skills Practiced

Active listening

Concentration

Coordination

Time Frame

3–4 minutes

Materials

Optional: Copies of Fidget Family story, chart paper, or whiteboard

Variation

Write new Fidget Family stories by retelling a historical event or incorporating key concepts and vocabulary words from your unit of study.

How to Do It

1 **Assign students different characters** from the story on the opposite page. Delete or add characters as necessary, or assign more than one student to a character.

2 **The leader reads the story aloud** at a quick pace. When students hear their part read, they stand up, twirl around once, and sit back down.

3 **When the leader reads the phrase "Fidget Family,"** everyone stands, twirls around once (or does another action), and sits back down.

Tips for Success

➤ As needed, teach and model how to move safely and quietly and to be respectful of others nearby. (See p. 7 for Interactive Modeling steps.)

➤ Share strategies on how to listen for each part—the story moves quickly! You may also want to give students a copy of the story or display it on chart paper or whiteboard.

Fidget Family

Characters

Ma
Pa
Billy
Tommy
Bridget
Baby
Grandma
Grandpa
Old Mol
Old Dol
cat
dog
canary
gate
tree
road
house
wagon
blanket

Once upon a time, there was a family called the Fidget Family. There were lots of people in this family. There were Ma Fidget, Pa Fidget, Billy Fidget, Tommy Fidget, Bridget Fidget, and Baby Fidget. They had several pets. They had a cat, a dog, a canary, and two horses named Old Mol and Old Dol. Through the gate, past a tree, and down the road in another house lived Grandma and Grandpa Fidget.

One day, the whole Fidget Family decided to go visit Grandma and Grandpa Fidget at their house through the gate, past the tree, and down the road. Billy wanted to bring the cat, Tommy wanted to bring the dog, and Bridget wanted to bring the canary, but Ma and Pa Fidget said no. Baby Fidget cried. So they loaded up the wagon, hitched up Old Mol and Old Dol, and headed out through the gate, past the tree, and down the road to Grandma and Grandpa Fidget's house. They had just passed the tree when Baby cried again. The whole Fidget Family realized they'd left Baby's blanket back at the house. Baby kept crying.

So the whole Fidget Family turned the wagon around, and Old Mol and Old Dol pulled the wagon back up the road, past the tree, and through the gate. They finally found Baby's blanket back at the house. Before they left, Billy asked if he could bring the cat, Tommy wanted to bring the dog, and Bridget wanted to bring the canary, but Ma and Pa Fidget said no. Baby started chewing on the blanket.

Then the whole Fidget Family got back into the wagon being pulled by Old Mol and Old Dol. They rode out through the gate, past the tree, and down the road to Grandma and Grandpa Fidget's house. They had a wonderful time, and the whole Fidget Family lived happily ever after!

The Four Elements

In Brief

Quiet body and mind with peaceful words and motions.

Skills Practiced

Concentration

Coordination

Self-awareness

Time Frame

1–3 minutes

Materials

None

Variation

For an invigorating activity, the leader performs lively movements (such as clapping hands or slapping thighs) and speeds up as each new motion is introduced.

How to Do It

1 **Students sit at their desks** or in a circle, so that everyone can see the leader.

2 **The leader begins by chanting** "Earth, air, fire, water . . ." while making a simple motion (such as raising arms sideways over the head until palms meet).

3 **The group joins in the chant** and imitates the leader's motion. After repeating the chant once or twice, the leader changes to a different motion and does it more slowly than the previous one. Everyone copies the new motion while continuing to chant.

4 **The leader continues changing the motions** and slowing down with each change until the final motion: hands folded on lap. The activity ends with a few moments of silence.

Tip for Success

➤ Brainstorm different movements the leader can do for Steps 3 and 4.

B R A I N   B I T
When students feel less stressed, they're better able to focus on improving their academic and social-emotional skills.

Group Charades

In Brief

Incorporate vocabulary practice into a classic guessing game.

Skills Practiced

Brainstorming

Creative thinking

Inferring/interpreting

Teamwork

Time Frame

3–7 minutes

Materials

Index cards

Variations

Let students choose the vocabulary words or phrases to act out.

Have individuals act out within their small groups or for the whole class.

How to Do It

1 **Students form groups** of three or four. Give each group an index card (prepared in advance) on which you've written a vocabulary word or familiar academic phrase.

2 **Give groups a minute or so** to figure out how they'll act out their word or phrase. Emphasize that all group members are expected to participate.

3 **Each group then acts out** their word or phrase while the rest of the class guesses. Or choose two or three groups and schedule the others for successive class periods.

Tips for Success

➤ As needed, model and practice these silent charade signals:

- Hold up fingers to show number of words.

- Hold up fingers to show first word, second word, etc.

- Lay fingers on forearm to show number of syllables.

- Pull ear lobe to indicate "sounds like."

- Point to nose and then to person who guessed something correctly.

➤ Decide how students will guess; for example, they might raise hands to be called on by the actors.

Hands Up!

In Brief

Quickly recall information while clapping and chanting.

Skills Practiced

Active listening

Concentration

Coordination

Recalling/retaining information

Time Frame

2–5 minutes

Materials

Chart paper or whiteboard

Variation

Invite students to come up with categories themselves.

How to Do It

1 **Name a category** related to something students are learning; they'll insert the category name into the fourth line of the chant.

2 **Students stand at their desks** or sit in a circle. Display the words on chart paper or whiteboard and chant them together while doing the accompanying motions:

"Hands up"	(put both hands up)
"For 20___"	(change to current year)
"Gonna name"	(clap, clap)
"Some [category]"	(clap, clap)
"One apiece"	(clap, clap)
"No repeats"	(clap, clap)
"No hesitation"	(clap, clap)
"No duplication"	(clap, clap)
"Starting with"	(clap, clap)
"[Student's name]"	(clap, clap)
_____	(student says something that fits the category)
(Pause)	(clap, clap)

3 **Keep clapping and repeating the last three lines** until everyone has had a turn. Do as many rounds and categories as time allows.

Tip for Success

➤ Discuss what to do if someone makes a mistake, such as giving them another chance or whispering a suggestion to them while everyone keeps the beat going with their clapping.

Have a Ball

In Brief

Mimic how the leader tosses and catches a paper ball.

Skills Practiced

Concentration
Coordination

Time Frame

1–2 minutes

Materials

Scrap paper

Variation

For added challenge, time students to see how quickly they can complete the actions. With each round, they can try to beat the class record.

How to Do It

1 **Students sit at their desks** and crumple a piece of scrap paper into a ball.

2 **The leader sits in a chair facing the class** and does various actions with the paper ball; students copy each action. Sample actions (all done while seated):

- Place the ball on top of your feet (feet together) and repeatedly toss the ball up and catch it with your feet.

- Set the ball on your left elbow. Flip the ball into the air and catch it with your left hand. Switch sides.

- With your hands, toss the ball backwards over your head and move your hands behind your back to catch it.

- With your feet slightly apart, lift your legs one at a time and use one hand and then the other as you weave the ball over and under the right and left legs in a figure eight pattern.

3 **To conclude,** students toss their ball into a recycle bin. If they miss, they simply pick it up and place it in the bin.

Tip for Success

➤ Encourage students to help each other out if a paper ball goes astray.

Humdingers

In Brief

Hum one of four songs while seeking others who are humming the same song.

Skills Practiced

Concentration

Differentiating

Teamwork

Time Frame

1–3 minutes

Materials

Small pieces of paper

Pen or pencil

Variation

Brainstorm a list of pop songs and randomly choose four to use.

How to Do It

1 **Write the titles** of four different, very common songs (such as current pop songs or childhood songs like "Itsy Bitsy Spider") on small pieces of paper. Write enough slips for each title so that students can form four equal groups. (It's OK if a group has one member more or less than the other groups.) Randomly distribute the slips, one per student.

2 **While students hum their song,** they move safely about the room listening for others who are humming the same song.

3 **When students find a match,** they stand together and hum the song in unison until four groups have formed, each humming a different song.

4 **End the activity** with each group humming their song while others guess its name.

Tips for Success

➤ Model and practice humming at a middle volume range— neither too loud nor too soft—so everyone can hear one another. (See p. 7 for Interactive Modeling steps.)

➤ Remind students to spread out as they mix and mingle so that everyone has enough space to walk around the room.

B R A I N   B I T

Music can improve students' moods, reduce stress, and help modulate energy levels.

Imagine This

In Brief

Build a detailed mental image through guided meditation.

Skills Practiced

Active listening

Concentration

Visualization

Time Frame

1–2 minutes

Materials

None

Variations

Play quiet, soothing music to help students focus on visualizing.

Instead of naming an object or setting in Step 2, the leader briefly holds up a photo (such as one from pp. 89–95). Students examine the photo for a few moments before closing eyes and imagining.

How to Do It

1 **Students stand by their desks** and perform a few simple movements—they might stretch their arms up over their heads and lift first one leg and then the other.

2 **Students sit back down and close their eyes.** The leader begins by saying "Imagine this" and names an object or setting, such as "evergreen forest." Students visualize this image, keeping eyes closed and remaining silent.

3 **After 10 seconds or so,** the leader calls on a student. The student adds a detail, such as "a blue jay on a pine branch."

4 **The leader gives everyone a few seconds** to visualize this detail and then calls on the next student who adds another detail, such as "gently falling rain." Continue as time allows.

Tips for Success

➤ Discuss appropriate images to share. Go over what it means to create a mental image and share strategies for how to keep eyes closed.

➤ If closing eyes is uncomfortable for some students, make it optional. Students may also rest their heads on their desks to help them concentrate.

Interruptions

In Brief

Unwind by making punctuation sounds as a poem or passage is read aloud.

Skills Practiced

Active listening

Concentration

Deep breathing

Time Frame

1–2 minutes

Materials

Copies of a short poem or prose passage, or chart paper or whiteboard

Variation

For increased energy, make sounds such as "shoom-bop!" and do active movements (jump up at the beginning of a sentence; sit down at the end).

How to Do It

1 **Students stand by their desks,** perform a few simple movements (for example, twisting side to side with hands on hips), and sit back down.

2 **The leader reads the chosen text aloud** as students say soothing words or make sounds for each type of punctuation (or other text elements such as stanza breaks or vocabulary words). For example:

Exclamation point	"Ha" (or exhale loudly)
Period	"Ah" (or exhale softly)
Comma	"Huh" (or breathe out a puff of air)
Question mark	"Hmmm" (or inhale and exhale quickly while raising and then dropping shoulders in a shrug)

3 **When the leader finishes reading,** students take a few slow, deep breaths.

Tip for Success

➤ Post the sounds or actions on an anchor chart that everyone can see.

In the Bag

In Brief

Visualize "balling up" excess energy or worry and "throwing it away."

Skills Practiced

Concentration

Deep breathing

Self-awareness

Visualization

Time Frame

1–2 minutes

Materials

None

Variation

Students visualize all the positives in their lives and put these in an infinitely expandable bag that they carry with them for support throughout the week.

How to Do It

1 **Students stand in a circle** or sit at their desks. Tell them to imagine that they have an "infinitely expandable" bag, such as a shopping bag, gym bag, or suitcase.

2 **Brainstorm stressors and worries** students may have, such as negative thoughts, conflicts, or test anxiety.

3 **Students close their eyes and then visualize** compressing any tension or stressors into one or more imaginary balls. Remind them that they can make the ball(s) any size they want because their bag is expandable.

4 **On your signal,** students visualize tossing the ball(s) into their bag and then throwing the bag away.

5 **Tell them to now think** about a place (real or imaginary) where they feel safe and at peace. After a short pause, everyone takes some slow, deep breaths by inhaling through the nose for a count of five, holding it in for two seconds, and then exhaling through the mouth for a few seconds. Repeat two or three times.

Tips for Success

➤ If needed, model and practice how to do deep breathing. (See p. 7 for Interactive Modeling steps.)

➤ If students prefer not to close their eyes, they can rest their heads on their desks to help them concentrate.

Just Like Me!

In Brief

Make personal connections by seeing who responds to the leader's statements.

Skills Practiced

Active listening

Making personal connections

Self-awareness

Understanding multiple perspectives

Time Frame

1–3 minutes

Materials

None

Variations

Say "Just like me" in other languages.

Invite other (school-appropriate) responses, such as "I second that!" "Ditto!" or "Simpatico!"

How to Do It

1 **The leader stands at the front** of the classroom or in the center of the circle. Everyone else sits.

2 **The leader makes a positive statement,** such as "I aced math class today," "I'm looking forward to school vacation," or "I like to read." Everyone to whom the statement applies stands up and says "Just like me!" and then sits down again.

3 **The leader makes another statement,** and group members again respond. Continue through a number of statements as time allows.

Tips for Success

➤ Discuss with students what information is appropriate to share in class.

➤ To help students make personal connections, emphasize that they should also pay attention to who stands after statements are made.

B R A I N   B I T
Repetition helps create long-term memories, which students can then recall and apply to new learning.

Let It Rain

Imitate storm sounds—
high energy of thunder,
calmness of rain.

Skills Practiced

Concentration

Coordination

Teamwork

Time Frame

2–4 minutes

Materials

None

Variation

Point to a new group for
each action—you'll need
seven groups. Each group
continues its sound as
the next group begins
theirs. In reverse, each
group stops their action
when you point to them.

How to Do It

1 **Students stand in a circle** or stay seated. The leader says, "I'm the storm maestro. When I do an action, copy me, and we'll replicate a rainstorm together."

2 **Without talking, the storm maestro leads** students through the rainstorm as it builds—and then challenges everyone to make the rain get softer as the storm dies down, as follows:

As the Storm Builds

Rub hands on thighs	(light wind)
Rub hands together	(stronger wind)
Snap fingers	(soft rain)
Clap hands softly	(hard rain)
Clap hands loudly	(pouring rain)
Slap thighs loudly	(soft thunder)
Stomp feet	(loud thunder)

As the Storm Dies Down

Stomp feet
Slap thighs loudly
Clap hands loudly
Clap hands softly
Snap fingers
Rub hands together
Rub hands on thighs

Tip for Success

➤ Start off slowly the first few times and pick up speed as students become more familiar with the actions.

Love It or Leave It

In Brief

Learn about each other as everyone practices "on the spot" decision-making.

Skills Practiced

Active listening

Categorizing

Making personal connections

Understanding multiple perspectives

Time Frame

1–3 minutes

Materials

None

Variation

Designate one side of the room as "Love it" and the other as "Leave it." Students stand in a line in the middle of the room; the leader calls out a topic. Students step to the side of their choice, see who else is in their group, and then move back to the center for the next round.

How to Do It

1 **The leader names a topic,** such as a movie, TV show, book, or song, and then says "Love it or leave it?"

2 **Going in turn, students throw their arms up** in the air as they say "Love it" or stomp feet as they say "Leave it," depending on whether they like or dislike what the leader named. This activity works best when students react quickly rather than taking time to ponder. Repeat with a new topic.

Tip for Success

➤ Explain that students must choose one of the two responses. If they have mixed feelings about the topic named, they should choose the response that is *most* true for them.

Ma Zinga

In Brief

Build up and then release energy with a team cheer!

Skills Practiced

Concentration

Coordination

Self-awareness

Teamwork

Time Frame

1 minute

Materials

None

Variation

Instead of "Ma Zinga," create new phrases to say.

How to Do It

1 **Students stand** with their arms pointing straight into the middle of the circle (or stand by their desks and point toward the front of the room). Choose a student to be the leader or ask for a volunteer.

2 **The group says "Ma-a-a-a . . ."** with the "ah" sound gradually rising as students shake their fingers, hands, and arms to build up energy and a sense of team spirit.

3 **At the leader's signal**—a nod of the head—the group quickly pulls back their hands while forming fists and cheers "Zinga!" loudly together. This motion pulls all that great team spirit and energy back into each individual.

4 **Repeat with a new leader** as time allows.

Tips for Success

➤ Ask students to imagine how building up team spirit and positive energy might look, sound, and feel—for example, they might look alert or excited, sound happy, or feel more energized the longer they hold the "Ma-a-a-a."

➤ Encourage students to imagine letting go of any negative thoughts as they stretch their arms out and then imagine pulling in positive thoughts as they bring their arms back in.

Mellow Echo

In Brief

Follow simple motions to focus on the present moment.

Skills Practiced

Active listening

Concentration

Deep breathing

Self-awareness

Time Frame

1–2 minutes

Materials

None

Variation

To recharge students, the leader does vigorous movements, such as jumping jacks or running in place.

How to Do It

1 **Students stand or sit at their desks.** The leader performs slow motions, poses, or stretches while naming them. Students echo what the leader says while imitating the motions. For example:

"Breathe in and look up toward the sky . . ." (lift head up)

"Breathe out and look down to the earth . . ." (move head down)

"Stretch to the right and breathe in and out . . ." (roll head to right shoulder; hold)

"Stretch to the left and breathe in and out . . ." (roll head to left shoulder; hold)

2 **The leader continues with other calming motions** for students to follow.

3 **After repeating the sequence two or three times,** the leader concludes with a few deep breaths; students do the same.

Tip for Success

➤ Talk about how slow movements and quiet voices help to refresh body and mind.

B R A I N   B I T
Breathing exercises and simple movements can help refresh the brain and enhance learning.

Metaphorical Connections

In Brief

Make creative connections between everyday objects and academic content.

Skills Practiced

Clear speaking

Creative thinking

Inferring/interpreting

Time Frame

2–4 minutes

Materials

Any common object in the classroom

Variations

Form pairs or small groups to brainstorm metaphors.

Instead of using an object, display a picture, such as one of the photos on pp. 89–95.

For an energy boosting activity, students pop up as they state their metaphor.

How to Do It

1 **Students stand by their desks,** perform a few simple movements (stretching, jogging in place), and then sit down.

2 **The leader holds up an object** and asks how it might relate to academic content. For example: "How is a rubber band a metaphor for math?"

3 **Students have a minute or so** to think about possible connections and then generate a metaphor.

4 **The leader says "Time"** and calls on students as they raise their hands. Metaphors may be serious or silly. For example:

Student 1: "Math stretches our memory."

Student 2: "Math snaps us to attention."

Student 3: "Math holds all the parts of equations together."

5 **Repeat with a new object and question** as time allows.

Tips for Success

➤ Define "metaphor" and give examples. You might explain: "A metaphor is a figure of speech that connects two unrelated things without using 'like' or 'as.' For example: A typewriter is a dinosaur." (Connects older technology to an extinct animal.)

➤ Discuss ways that students can support each other if they get confused or don't understand a metaphor that's shared.

Mirrors

In Brief

Mirror a partner's calm movements to slow down body and mind.

Skills Practiced

Concentration

Coordination

Creative thinking

Teamwork

Time Frame

1–2 minutes

Materials

Chime or other instrument that makes a soothing sound

Variations

For an energizing activity, students speed up each time they switch roles to see if they can keep up with their partner.

For a whole-group activity, the leader faces the classroom; everyone else stands at their desk and mirrors the leader's motions.

How to Do It

1 **Students stand, face a partner,** and decide who will lead first and who will follow.

2 **The leader begins** by making slow and steady motions—without speaking—while the follower mirrors the movements.

3 **After 15–30 seconds, ring the chime** (or use some other soothing sound). Students switch roles. Repeat as time allows.

Tips for Success

➤ Brainstorm, model, and practice various motions that can be performed slowly and steadily. (See p. 7 for Interactive Modeling steps.) If needed, discuss school-appropriate movements, such as bending from side to side and shrugging shoulders.

➤ Remind students to move at a steady pace, and challenge them to synchronize their movements with their partner's.

Never-Ending Word

In Brief

Think and respond quickly with this fast-moving word game.

Skills Practiced

Active listening

Building vocabulary

Categorizing

Recalling/retaining information

Time Frame

1–3 minutes

Materials

Optional: Chart paper or whiteboard

Variations

Incorporate some challenges, such as "no repeats" or saying the next word within five seconds.

Use a timer to challenge students to beat their previous records of words said in the allotted timespan.

How to Do It

1 **The leader calls out a category** related to academic content or something personal (such as favorite foods) and then says a word associated with the category.

2 **When a student thinks of a word** that fits into that category and starts with the last letter of the previous word said, the student pops up and says the word. For example:

> Leader: "The category is chemical elements: Phosphorus!"
>
> Student 1: "Sulphur!"
>
> Student 2: "Radon!"
>
> Student 3: "Nickel!"

Optional: The leader writes down the category and the words that are called out on chart paper or whiteboard.

3 **Once students pop up,** they remain standing until everyone has had a turn.

4 **The brain break ends** when the whole class is standing or time runs out.

Tip for Success

➤ Talk about how to support each other if someone cannot think of a word or makes a mistake.

No Way!

In Brief

Take turns changing parts of a sentence with this version of Telephone.

Skills Practiced

Active listening

Clear speaking

Concentration

Creative thinking

Time Frame

2–4 minutes

Materials

Chart paper or whiteboard

Variations

For a greater challenge, rely on memory: the leader says the original sentence but does not write it down.

The leader creates the original sentence after looking at an image (such as one on pp. 89–95) and then displays the image where everyone can see it.

How to Do It

1 **On chart paper or whiteboard,** the leader writes a sentence that gives several pieces of information about an activity, such as who did what, when, where, and with whom.

2 **Students then take turns** changing just one element of the sentence until everyone has had a turn and the original sentence has completely changed. The leader makes the edits on the chart paper or whiteboard. For example:

> Original sentence: "Last weekend, my cousin Belinda and I went to the beach and we swam, collected shells, and went on a whale watch."

> First student: "No way! Last weekend, my *friend* Belinda and I went to the beach and we swam, collected shells, and went on a whale watch."

> Next student: "No way! Last weekend, my friend Belinda and I went to the beach and we swam, collected shells, and went **to an arcade**."

> Finally, the last sentence might be: "Yesterday, your brother Charlie and the ski club drove to the mountains where they hiked, drank hot chocolate, and practiced snowboarding tricks."

3 **The leader concludes with** "Oh, yeah! *That's* what happened!"

Tip for Success

➤ Discuss with students what types of activities are appropriate to talk about in school.

Number Freeze

In Brief

Work together to get a specified number of people standing at the same time.

Skills Practiced

Concentration

Mental math

Teamwork

Time Frame

1–3 minutes

Materials

Timer

Variation

Instead of getting a set number of students to stand, try to get a set number of students to hold a pose.

How to Do It

1 **Everyone begins seated.** The leader faces the class and calls out any number that's less than the size of the class.

2 **The leader sets the timer** for 60 seconds and says "Go!" Classmates try to get the stated number of people standing at the same time, while following these rules:

- No one may talk or point.

- Anyone may choose to stand at any time, but no one may stand for more than five seconds at a time (students count in their heads).

3 **When the leader thinks the right number of classmates is standing** (or when the timer goes off), the leader calls out "Freeze!" Students stay in their positions, and the leader counts the number of people standing to see if the numbers match.

4 **Repeat as time allows;** switch leaders each time the numbers match or after each round.

Tips for Success

➤ Invite the class to brainstorm strategies for guesstimating the correct number silently.

➤ Discuss ways that students can count to five in their heads without getting distracted, such as silently counting on their fingers or mouthing the numbers.

Password

In Brief

Brainstorm synonyms for a chosen word in this classic TV show spin-off.

Skills Practiced

Brainstorming

Categorizing

Recalling/retaining information

Teamwork

Time Frame

2–4 minutes

Materials

Chart paper or whiteboard

Timer

Variation

Students form small groups with one group member as the Contestant. The Contestant closes their eyes or rests their head on the desk while the rest of the group silently chooses the password and writes down clue words.

How to Do It

1 **Display a list of vocabulary words** on chart paper or whiteboard.

2 **Choose a student to be the Contestant;** that student leaves the room and stands in the hallway. Everyone else remains seated.

3 **The rest of the class selects a word** from the list (the password). Set the timer for 60 seconds; students brainstorm clues they can give to help the Contestant guess correctly.

4 **The Contestant returns** and calls on 3–5 students for clues. For example, if the class chooses the password "vocation," students might offer the synonyms "trade," "talent," or "calling" as clues. After 3–5 clues, the Contestant says "The password is [guessed word]."

5 **Regardless of whether the Contestant guesses correctly,** students drum their hands on their desks or rapidly stomp their feet (to mimic the sound of a drumroll) and then say in unison "The password is [chosen word]."

6 **If time permits, the Contestant chooses** a student to become the next Contestant.

B R A I N   B I T
Brain breaks can help the brain coordinate its reasoning and emotional functions, which can boost students' academic and social-emotional learning.

Tips for Success

➤ Model and practice, as needed, how to safely and gently drum hands and stomp feet at an appropriate volume and intensity level. (See p. 7 for Interactive Modeling steps.)

➤ Brainstorm with students how to give synonyms (or brief definitions) for a word without using any variation of the word in the definition.

➤ When first introducing this game, you may want to allow the Contestant to have two or three guesses.

If the password is VOCATION . . .

A synonym for the password is CALLING

Peaceful Reading

In Brief

Listen to soothing words read aloud.

Skills Practiced

Active listening

Inferring/interpreting

Making personal connections

Self-awareness

Time Frame

2–3 minutes

Materials

Short poem or prose passage

Variation

For a rejuvenating activity, the leader (or the whole class) reads at a faster pace while everyone does some energetic actions.

How to Do It

1 **Students stand by their desks,** perform a few simple movements (simple stretching, jogging in place), and then sit back down.

2 **Choose a descriptive or peaceful piece** for the leader to read aloud, such as one of the poems on the opposite page (or check out the sample reading list on p. 70).

3 **After the reading,** invite a few student volunteers to discuss how they felt or what they visualized as they listened to the piece.

Tip for Success

➤ Encourage students to visualize images and emotions that the text evokes as they listen.

Peaceful Reading

Spring Storm

BY WILLIAM CARLOS WILLIAMS

The sky has given over
its bitterness.
Out of the dark change
all day long
rain falls and falls
as if it would never end.
Still the snow keeps
its hold on the ground.
But water, water
from a thousand runnels!
It collects swiftly,
dappled with black
cuts a way for itself
through green ice in the gutters.
Drop after drop it falls
from the withered grass-stems
of the overhanging embankment.

Luck Is Not Chance

BY EMILY DICKINSON

Luck is not chance—
It's Toil—
Fortune's expensive smile
Is earned—
The Father of the Mine
Is that old-fashioned Coin
We spurned—

When I Rise Up

BY GEORGIA DOUGLAS JOHNSON

When I rise up above the earth,
And look down on the things
   that fetter me,
I beat my wings upon the air,
Or tranquil lie,
Surge after surge of potent
   strength
Like incense comes to me
When I rise up above the earth
And look down upon the things
   that fetter me.

Picture This

In Brief

Envision a favorite activity to relax and create a positive mood.

Skills Practiced

Concentration

Creative thinking

Visualization

Time Frame

1–2 minutes

Materials

None

Variations

Students envision themselves successfully meeting a challenge, such as doing well on a test, performing at a musical concert, or surpassing a personal record at an athletic event.

Pass around a photo (such as one of the photos on pp. 89–95) or display one where everyone can see; invite students to imagine themselves in the picture.

How to Do It

1 **Students stand by their desks** and do a few simple movements, such as stretching arms overhead and "shaking out" legs, and then sit back down.

2 **Tell students to take a deep breath** and close their eyes. Then guide them through the following visualization:

> "Think about something you really like doing. It could be walking your dog, hanging out with a friend—anything that makes you happy . . .

> "Imagine yourself doing this activity . . . What do you see? . . . What do you hear? . . . What do you feel?

> "Now imagine that it's time to end the activity . . . As you wrap it up, you feel peaceful, relaxed . . ."

3 **Give students a few moments to end their visualizations;** then say "On three, open your eyes. One, two, three."

4 **Ask volunteers to share** what they visualized, as time allows.

Tip for Success

➤ If closing eyes is uncomfortable for some students, make it optional. Students may rest their heads on their desks or look at a picture instead (see photos on pp. 89–95).

B R A I N   B I T
Students are more likely to be successful when they can visualize success.

Pros and Cons

In Brief

Take turns quickly listing pros and cons of a topic with a partner.

Skills Practiced

Active listening

Clear speaking

Recalling/retaining information

Understanding multiple perspectives

Time Frame

2–3 minutes

Materials

Timer

Variations

Announce topics ahead of time and brainstorm a few ideas as a class before students pair up.

Students generate their own topics.

How to Do It

1 **Assign partners.** Students find a space in the room where they can sit or stand together. Each pair decides who calls out first (A) and who responds (B). Announce the first topic (for example, wind power, energy drinks, video games). Give students some think time; then signal them to begin and set the timer for 20 seconds.

2 **Student A claps her hands** and says "Pro!" Student B quickly names pros, or positive points, about the topic. After 20 seconds, signal students to stop.

3 **Student A claps her hands again** and says "Con!" Student B now names cons, or negative points, about the topic. After 20 seconds, signal again to end this round.

4 **Students keep the same partners** but switch roles. You can use the same topic or choose a new one. Repeat as time allows.

5 **After the final round,** briefly review as a class some of the pros and cons that were shared.

Tips for Success

➤ Start with general or neutral topics before using more complex or challenging topics.

➤ If some students struggle with or feel too anxious about the activity, slow the pace and allow more time for each round.

Relax, Breathe, Repeat

In Brief

Ease mind and body with deep breathing and slow movements.

Skills Practiced

Concentration

Deep breathing

Self-awareness

Time Frame

2–3 minutes

Materials

Chime or other instrument that makes a soothing sound

Variation

Brainstorm other simple stretches and movements to accompany the breathing.

How to Do It

1 **Students stand at their desks** or in a circle. Ring a chime (or use another soothing sound). Students close their eyes and focus on the sound. When the sound stops, students inhale slowly and deeply and then exhale slowly. They continue this slow, deep breathing for about 30 seconds.

2 **Ring the chime again.** Students continue slow, deep breathing until the sound ends. They open their eyes and remain still and quiet for a silent count of five.

3 **Ring the chime again.** Students extend their arms in front of them with their fingertips touching as if holding a large pumpkin.

4 **Students stretch their arms wide** as they inhale to the count of five and then bring arms back in until fingertips touch again (as if holding the pumpkin) while exhaling to the count of five. Repeat five times.

5 **Students rest their arms at their sides.** Then they take a slow, deep breath, bring their shoulders up to their ears, and exhale as they release their shoulders.

Tips for Success

➤ Make sure students have enough space to stretch their arms.

➤ Model and practice how to do slow, deep breathing and the accompanying stretch. (See p. 7 for Interactive Modeling steps.)

Shake It Down

In Brief

Follow the leader's rhythmic actions to release tension and boost alertness.

Skills Practiced

Concentration

Coordination

Mental math

Time Frame

1–2 minutes

Materials

None

Variation

In a circle, while shaking right hand, students place left hand gently on the shoulder of the person to their left. Then they switch sides.

How to Do It

1 **Students stand by their desks** or in a circle. The leader takes them through the following chant and actions:

"1, 2, 3, 4, 5, 6, 7, 8, 9, 10, 11, 12, 13, 14, 15, 16!"
(Lift right hand up and shake it sixteen times. Repeat with left hand, right foot, left foot.)

"Cut!"
(Pretend to slice or cut right hand down on left palm.)

"1, 2, 3, 4, 5, 6, 7, 8!"
(Lift right hand up and shake it eight times. Repeat with left hand, right foot, left foot.)

"Cut!"
(Pretend to slice or cut right hand down on left palm.)

2 **Repeat the chant and actions** cutting down to 4, then 2, and finally 1.

3 **To conclude:**

"Shake it down!"
(Shake whole body once from top to bottom!)

Tip for Success

➤ Discuss strategies for maintaining balance and self-control while staying in place.

Shanti Om

In Brief

Chant while repeating simple motions that promote a "peaceful state of being."

Skills Practiced

Concentration

Coordination

Self-awareness

Time Frame

1–2 minutes

Materials

None

Variation

Try other simple motions or relaxation poses, such as:

Crescent Moon (raise arms overhead with palms touching; bend left at waist and reach upward; then bend right and reach upward)

Tree (raise arms overhead with palms touching; stand on left leg and lift right leg with knee bent; rotate bent knee to the right while pressing sole of right foot against side of left thigh, calf, or ankle)

How to Do It

1 **Students stand by their desks** or in a circle. Everyone repeats the following words and motions with the leader, moving on the emphasized words shown in bold below.

| Pronunciation | **Shanti:** shŏn-tē |
| | **Om:** ōm |

Words	**Shanti** Shanti **Om**
	Shanti **Om**
	Shanti **Om**

Motions

Round One:	Move hands left, then right.
Round Two:	Clap hands gently on thighs.
Round Three:	Take one step left and one step right.
Round Four:	Touch the floor and then reach for the sky.

2 **Repeat as time allows,** introducing a new motion with each round.

3 **Conclude with one long "O-o-o-m-m-m"** while standing still with arms resting at sides.

Tip for Success

➤ Tell students that Shanti Om is generally interpreted as meaning "a peaceful state of being."

Silent Card Trade

In Brief

Create tranquil mental images from words or photos.

Skills Practiced

Concentration

Visualization

Time Frame

1–2 minutes

Materials

Silent Card Trade handouts (pp. 71–82) or other cards or slips of paper with calming images or words (such as ocean waves or rain forest)

Chime or other instrument that makes a soothing sound

Variation

Conclude by asking for student volunteers to share one thing they visualized.

How to Do It

1 **Give each student a Silent Card Trade handout** (pp. 71–82) or use your own image or word handouts.

2 **Allow 5–10 seconds** for everyone to examine their word or image.

3 **Ring the chime** (or use another soothing sound). Students close their eyes and silently visualize the word or image.

4 **After 10–20 seconds,** ring the chime again. Students open their eyes and then silently exchange cards with someone nearby. Repeat Steps 2–4 as time allows.

Tips for Success

➤ As a class, discuss some strategies for visualizing, such as thinking of related words or focusing on a detail in the image.

➤ If students feel uncomfortable closing their eyes, they can practice visualizing with their eyes open as they look at their card.

Silent Quotes

In Brief

Silently find the person who has the other half of a quote.

Skills Practiced

Inferring/interpreting

Making personal connections

Time Frame

1–3 minutes

Materials

Silent Quotes handouts (pp. 83–88) or slips of paper with quotes

Variation

Instead of doing Steps 4–5, each pair shares their quote with the class.

How to Do It

1 **Use the Silent Quotes handouts** (pp. 83–88) or make your own (include the name of the person being quoted on each half so students can more easily find their matches). For example:

From *Through the Looking Glass and What Alice Found There* by Lewis Carroll:

> **Strip One** "Why, sometimes I've believed as many as . . .
> THE WHITE QUEEN

> **Strip Two** . . . six impossible things before breakfast."
> THE WHITE QUEEN

2 **Mix up the half-quotes** and pass one to each student.

3 **Students read their half of the quote to themselves** and then silently move around the room searching for their match.

4 **Once students find their matching partner,** they briefly talk about the quote's meaning or share a personal connection to it.

5 **If time allows,** invite a few pairs to share their full quote with the class.

Tip for Success

➤ If you have an odd number of students, either cut one quote into three strips or include yourself as one of the matches.

Snap Wink

In Brief

Practice hand-eye coordination—simple yet challenging.

Skills Practiced

Concentration

Coordination

Time Frame

1–2 minutes

Materials

None

Variation

For an advanced version, pinch left ear with right hand and press nose with left hand. When the leader says "Pinch Press!" switch sides. With each round, the leader increases the speed.

How to Do It

1 **Students stand at their desks** or in a circle. Starting slowly and increasing speed, everyone winks their left eye and snaps the fingers on their right hand.

2 **The leader calls out "Snap Wink!"** Instantly, everyone winks their right eye and snaps the fingers on their left hand.

3 **Repeat three or four times,** going faster each time.

4 **To conclude,** the leader calls out "Break!" and everyone sits down.

Tip for Success

➤ Brainstorm ways students can encourage each other during this activity.

B R A I N   B I T
Providing healthy outlets for stress is especially beneficial for young adolescents' growth and development.

Solar Power

In Brief

Visualize the warmth and energy of the sun.

Skills Practiced

Active listening

Deep breathing

Self-awareness

Visualization

Time Frame

2–4 minutes

Materials

None

Variation

Do this activity outside.

How to Do It

1 **Students stand at their desks** or in a circle and take a few slow, deep breaths.

2 **Everyone closes their eyes** while the leader takes the class through this guided visualization:

"Imagine the sun is just above you. Visualize the sun's light and energy slowly filling your head, then moving gently into your neck, spreading into your shoulders . . . your arms . . . your hands . . . your legs . . . your feet . . . Imagine the warm and gentle light filling your whole body . . .

"Now imagine the sun's warmth and light shining out of you . . . [Skip to **Conclusion** for a shorter version.]

"Through your eyes . . . your fingers . . . your toes . . . and this light fills up the whole room . . . school . . . street . . . city . . . country . . . the whole world. Picture this warm light reaching up to the skies, filling the whole universe.

Conclusion: "Share the sun's light and energy—your own personal solar power—any time you want to relax or refocus . . . Now take a slow, deep breath . . . and open your eyes."

Tip for Success

➤ Share ideas about visualizing. For example, you might ask: "What helps you construct vivid pictures in your mind? How can creating positive mental images help people prepare for events that might be stressful, such as exams, sports tournaments, or performances?"

Soothing Sounds

In Brief

Calm the mind by imagining a soothing sound.

Skills Practiced

Concentration

Deep breathing

Self-awareness

Visualization

Time Frame

1–2 minutes

Materials

None

Variation

For a more energetic version, play recordings of sounds not easily recognized, such as paper being torn, and have students try to guess the sounds. Use your own recordings or those from a sound effects app or website.

How to Do It

1 **Students stand up,** do a few relaxing stretches or jumping jacks, and sit back down.

2 **Students take several slow, deep breaths** and close their eyes. Then the leader says:

> "Think about a sound you find soothing ... Imagine that you can just barely hear it far off in the distance ... Now the sound is closer and you can hear it a little bit louder ... closer still ...

> "Feel yourself relax as the sound fills your mind and your body ... Keep listening to the sound ... You feel calm and happy, as if you're floating on the sound ...

> "Now imagine that the sound is fading gradually into the distance ... fading ... fading ... You calmly let the sound go ... It's now silent ... You know you can bring this sound back and hear it in your head any time ... Now take a deep breath and slowly ... open ... your ... eyes."

3 **Ask volunteers to share** the sound they were imagining, as time allows.

Tips for Success

➤ Brainstorm soothing sounds, such as the sounds of nature, the hum of traffic, or the "whir" of a fan.

➤ If closing eyes is uncomfortable for some students, make it optional; they can rest their heads on their desks if that helps them concentrate, or simply sit quietly instead.

Switch

In Brief

Alternate thumbs up and finger pointing to challenge the brain.

Skills Practiced

Concentration

Coordination

Time Frame

1–2 minutes

Materials

None

Variations

Form pairs; take turns saying "Switch!"

Brainstorm other switches using hands, feet, legs, or arms.

How to Do It

1 **Students place their right hand out in front of them,** with the thumb up and all the fingers curled in. They place their left hand out in front of them, with their index finger out and the thumb and other fingers curled in.

2 **The leader calls out "Switch!"** Instantly, everyone switches the index fingers and thumbs of their hands so that the right hand now has the index finger pointing out and the left hand has the thumb up.

3 **On the next "Switch!"** the right hand will have the thumb up and the left will have the index finger pointing out. Continue alternating fingers and thumbs of both hands each time the leader calls out "Switch!"

Tips for Success

➤ Start off slowly and quicken the pace as students learn the motions.

➤ Discuss what respectful, encouraging words students can say to each other as they do this activity.

B R A I N   B I T
Reducing stress improves the brain's efficiency so that students can stay focused and learn more.

Three-Person Machine

In Brief

Team up and pantomime machines.

Skills Practiced

Coordination

Creative thinking

Inferring/interpreting

Teamwork

Time Frame

3–7 minutes

Materials

Chart paper or whiteboard

Variation

Have students demonstrate machines from the time periods they're studying or those used in other countries or cultures.

How to Do It

1 **Brainstorm different types of machines** or tools used in daily life. List ideas on chart paper or whiteboard.

2 **Students break into random (or assigned) groups** of three and model a machine or tool from the list. For example:

Car Wash

Two students stand a few feet apart and face each other. They act as the washer by raising hands overhead and wiggling their fingers to mimic water falling over the "car." The third student pantomimes driving the car while walking slowly between them.

3 **Each group demonstrates their machine** for the class to guess (or choose just one or two groups and have the others take their turns throughout the week).

Tips for Success

➤ Demonstrate one way to create a machine, such as the car wash example above.

➤ Tell students the expectations for how to guess each group's machine, such as by raising hands and waiting to be called on by the demonstrators.

Transformation

Transform into different beings in this version of Rock-Paper-Scissors.

Skills Practiced

Coordination

Teamwork

Time Frame

3–5 minutes

Materials

None

Variations

For a shorter version, end when the first student becomes Invincible.

Invite students to create their own set of beings, such as space creatures, superheroes, wizards, historical figures, or characters from a book.

How to Do It

1 **Explain that the four beings** in this version of Rock-Paper-Scissors transform as follows: Egg, Chicken, Dragon, Invincible. Only similar beings may play each other until they become Invincible.

2 **Everyone starts as an Egg,** finds a partner, and plays Rock-Paper-Scissors. The student who wins becomes a Chicken; the other student remains an Egg. Each being transforms up or down, accordingly, for each round.

3 **While looking for partners,** students can move as follows:

- Egg squats down.
- Chicken hunches with arms crooked like chicken wings.
- Dragon stands with arms outstretched, as if flying.
- Invincible stands tall with hands on hips, elbows pointing out from sides.

4 **Once students become Invincible,** they remain Invincible and can play against any being they want. If the other being wins the round, they also become Invincible. Play as long as time allows, or until everyone becomes Invincible.

Tip for Success

➤ Model and practice how to play Rock-Paper-Scissors. (See p. 7 for Interactive Modeling steps.)

Twisted Brain

In Brief

Follow the leader's twisty movements to rejuvenate body and mind.

Skills Practiced

Concentration

Coordination

Self-awareness

Time Frame

1–3 minutes

Materials

Chart paper or whiteboard

Variation

Have students create their own sequence of actions for everyone to follow.

How to Do It

1 **Students stand by their desks** or in a circle and follow along as the leader takes them through the following actions:

- Put hands out in front and clap—but miss (hands move past each other without touching). Then bring palms together and interlace fingers so that thumbs point down.

- Rotate hands so thumbs point up and pull arms inward until elbows are near sides.

- Roll shoulders to stretch back and neck.

- Cross right leg over left and roll neck clockwise. (Remind students to move carefully to maintain their balance.)

- Switch legs so left is over right and roll neck counterclockwise.

2 **Students return to their original standing position** with feet together and arms resting at sides. They close their eyes and silently spell their first name backwards and then their last name backwards.

Tip for Success

➤ Model and practice the actions beforehand as needed. (See p. 7 for Interactive Modeling steps.)

Watch It

In Brief

Keep multiple balls moving around the circle—everyone pay attention!

Skills Practiced

Concentration

Coordination

Teamwork

Time Frame

2–4 minutes

Materials

Two small balls made from soft material (such as rubber, yarn, or foam)

Variations

Once students master safely passing two balls all the way around the circle, add more (always use an even number).

Challenge students to pass two (or more) balls in opposite directions.

How to Do It

1 **Students stand in a circle** and count off by 2s.

2 **The 1s start by tossing a ball** around the circle, just to the 1s (skipping the student immediately beside them). Then the 2s start tossing a ball to the 2s. As students toss the ball, they say "Watch it!" and make eye contact with the student they're throwing the ball to. The student in between them ducks or steps out of the way.

3 **Students continue tossing** until both balls have gone completely around the circle and return to the students who first tossed them.

Tips for Success

➤ Emphasize that the expectation is to pass the balls efficiently and safely. (Using different colored balls makes it easier for students to track them.)

➤ As needed, model and practice how to gently toss the balls so that no one gets hit by mistake and everyone can easily catch the ball. (See p. 7 for Interactive Modeling steps.)

➤ Start off slowly and speed up as students become more skilled at moving the balls around the circle.

B R A I N   B I T
Combining movement with social interaction helps strengthen students' cognitive and social-emotional development.

Which Direction?

In Brief

Act as a "human compass" that turns in the direction the leader commands.

Skills Practiced

Active listening

Concentration

Inferring/interpreting

Time Frame

1–2 minutes

Materials

None

Variation

Incorporate exercise. For example:

"Stretch west and then reach northwest."

"Face southeast and do five jumping jacks."

How to Do It

1 **Students stand at their desks.** The leader starts by calling out simple directions, such as:

- "Everybody face south."
- "Now face northwest."

2 **Students quickly turn** to face the corresponding directions.

3 **Then the leader makes the directions more challenging:**

- "Face the direction where the sun would be at noon."
- "In which direction is the cafeteria?"
- "Turn so that you're facing downtown."

Tips for Success

➤ Post an anchor chart showing the compass directions.

➤ Start off slowly; quicken the pace as students become more familiar with the directions.

Woosha

In Brief

Try to choose different poses than the leader's in an upbeat guessing game.

Skills Practiced

Concentration

Coordination

Time Frame

1–2 minutes

Materials

None

Variation

Invite students to create their own set of three poses.

How to Do It

1 **Students stand by their desks.** The leader faces the class and says "One, two, three: Woosha!" and quickly does one of the following poses:

Fireball

Hold an imaginary ball in front of the body or off to the side.

Cobra

Bend arm up at the elbow and bend hand down to make a cobra head; rest the elbow on the back of the other hand.

Crane

Raise one leg up, bending at the knee; raise both hands above head.

2 **On "Woosha!"** students also assume one of the three poses, without waiting to see which pose the leader chooses.

3 **Anyone who does the same pose** as the leader sits down.

4 **The leader continues saying "One, two, three: Woosha!"** changing poses each time until only one person is left standing. That person becomes the new leader.

Tip for Success

➤ Demonstrate the three poses beforehand. Post an anchor chart of the poses if needed.

Word Storm

In Brief

Recall topic-related words as quickly as possible.

Skills Practiced

Brainstorming

Building vocabulary

Recalling/retaining information

Teamwork

Time Frame

2–4 minutes

Materials

Paper and pencils

Chart paper or whiteboard

Variations

Challenge students to use at least five of the words to create a humorous paragraph.

Instead of naming a topic, display a picture (such as one of the photos on pp. 89–95).

How to Do It

1 **Name a topic related to academic content** or something personal (for example, the American Revolution or favorite sports).

2 **Students count off to form small groups.** Assign or have students choose a recorder (note taker) to write down their group's ideas.

3 **Give groups one minute to brainstorm** words related to the topic. (For the American Revolution, words might include ally, tariff, boycott, Loyalist, blockade, allegiance.) The recorder lists all the words.

4 **When time is up,** call on each group one at a time to read their words while you (or a student volunteer) list them on chart paper or whiteboard. As other groups listen, the recorders cross off any words on their list that another group calls out.

5 **Repeat over the course of a unit of study,** challenging students to come up with more words related to the topic each time (or choose new topics).

Tips for Success

➤ For personal topics, discuss what's appropriate to share in school.

➤ Decide in advance what you'll do if a group offers a word unrelated to the topic. For example, you might say "Crackle" or "Kaboom!" then move the game along with an upbeat phrase, such as "Next storm!"

Zoom

In Brief

Send the word "Zoom" swiftly around the room.

Skills Practiced

Concentration

Coordination

Teamwork

Time Frame

1–2 minutes

Materials

Optional: Timer

Variation

With everyone seated in a circle, set a timer to one minute. Students then try to send the "Zoom!" around the circle as quickly as possible. Students can say "Eek!" to reverse the direction, but the goal is to get the "Zoom!" around the circle before time is up.

How to Do It

1 **Students begin seated** at their desks.

2 **The leader looks at an immediate neighbor** (someone sitting to the front, back, left, or right of them) and says "Zoom!" Then the leader stands up.

3 **The student who receives the "Zoom!"** quickly passes it to a neighbor and then stands up. This continues around the room with students saying "Zoom!" to a seated neighbor and then standing up.

4 **The activity finishes** when every student has had a chance to say "Zoom!" or when a student has no eligible (sitting) neighbors to "Zoom!"

Tip for Success

➤ Discuss what happens if a student has no eligible neighbors to "Zoom!" For example, everyone might sit back down and start the activity over with that student saying "Zoom!" first.

B R A I N   B I T
Brief breaks help adolescent brains respond in ways that can increase students' motivation.

Handouts

67

Tips for Using the Handouts

➤ The Silent Card Trade and Silent Quotes handouts may be cut out of the book or copied as needed. Also included are blank templates (Silent Card Trade pp. 77–78; Silent Quotes pp. 87–88) for you to copy to create your own handouts.

➤ The large photos on pages 89–95 may be displayed (where everyone can view them) or used as needed. These can be used with variations of:

- Encore Brainwriting, p. 23
- Imagine This, p. 31
- Metaphorical Connections, p. 39
- No Way!, p. 42
- Picture This, p. 48
- Word Storm, p. 65

Encore Brainwriting

SAMPLE READING LIST

Choose a passage from a text students are reading in class or from one of the following books:

I Will Always Write Back: How One Letter Changed Two Lives
    by Caitlin Alifirenka and Martin Ganda, with Liz Welch

Tuck Everlasting
    by Natalie Babbitt

Here's Looking at Euclid: From Counting Ants to Games of Chance—An Awe-Inspiring Journey Through the World of Numbers
    by Alex Bellos

Sahara Special
    by Esmé Raji Codell

Out of My Mind
    by Sharon M. Draper

The City of Ember
    by Jeanne DuPrau

90 Miles to Havana
    by Enrique Flores-Galbis

The Other Half of My Heart
    by Sundee T. Frazier

M.C. Higgins, the Great
    by Virginia Hamilton

Aquamarine
    by Alice Hoffman

The Boy Who Harnessed the Wind
    by William Kamkwamba and Bryan Mealer

Finding Audrey
    by Sophie Kinsella

The Giver
    by Lois Lowry

In the Footsteps of Crazy Horse
    by Joseph Marshall III, illustrated by Jim Yellowhawk

To Space and Back
    by Sally Ride, with Susan Okie

Uncle Tungsten: Memories of a Chemical Boyhood
    by Oliver Sacks

The Marvels
    by Brian Selznick

Space Chronicles: Facing the Ultimate Frontier
    by Neil deGrasse Tyson, edited by Avis Lang

A Time to Dance
    by Padma Venkatraman

The Martian
    by Andy Weir

Brown Girl Dreaming
    by Jacqueline Woodson

Acceptance

Calm

Celebration

Courage

Dedication

Friendship

Silent Card Trade

Responsive Classroom®

Silent Card Trade

Responsive Classroom®

Silent Card Trade

Responsive Classroom®

Silent Card Trade

Responsive Classroom®

Silent Card Trade

Responsive Classroom®

Silent Card Trade

Responsive Classroom®

Hope

Inspiration

Joy

Loyalty

Peace

Persistence

Silent Card Trade

Silent Card Trade

Responsive Classroom®

Silent Card Trade

Responsive Classroom®

Silent Card Trade

Responsive Classroom®

Silent Card Trade

Responsive Classroom®

Silent Card Trade

Responsive Classroom®

Silent Card Trade

Responsive Classroom®

Serenity

Strength

Success

TRUST

Warmth

Wisdom

Silent Card Trade

Silent Card Trade

Responsive Classroom®

Silent Card Trade

Silent Card Trade

Responsive Classroom®

Silent Card Trade

Silent Card Trade

Responsive Classroom®

Silent Card Trade

Silent Card Trade

Responsive Classroom®

Silent Card Trade

Silent Card Trade

Responsive Classroom®

Silent Card Trade

Silent Card Trade

Responsive Classroom®

Silent Card Trade

Silent Card Trade

Silent Card Trade
Responsive Classroom®

Silent Card Trade
Responsive Classroom®

Silent Card Trade
Responsive Classroom®

Silent Card Trade
Responsive Classroom®

Silent Card Trade
Responsive Classroom®

Silent Card Trade
Responsive Classroom®

Silent Card Trade

Silent Card Trade

Responsive Classroom®

Silent Card Trade

Responsive Classroom®

Silent Card Trade

Responsive Classroom®

Silent Card Trade

Responsive Classroom®

Silent Card Trade

Responsive Classroom®

Silent Card Trade

Responsive Classroom®

Silent Card Trade

Responsive Classroom®

Silent Card Trade

Responsive Classroom®

Silent Card Trade

Responsive Classroom®

Silent Card Trade

Responsive Classroom®

Silent Card Trade

Responsive Classroom®

Silent Card Trade

Responsive Classroom®

"Life is really simple . . .
CONFUCIUS

. . . but we insist on making it complicated."
CONFUCIUS

"My mission in life is not merely to survive, but to thrive . . .
MAYA ANGELOU

. . . and to do so with some passion, some compassion, some humor, and some style."
MAYA ANGELOU

"No act of kindness, no matter how small, . . .
AESOP

. . . is ever wasted."
AESOP

"Freedom is not worth having if . . .
MAHATMA GANDHI

. . . it does not include the freedom to make mistakes."
MAHATMA GANDHI

"Be sure you put your feet in the right place . . .
ABRAHAM LINCOLN

. . . then stand firm."
ABRAHAM LINCOLN

"The most courageous act is . . .
COCO CHANEL

. . . still to think for yourself. Aloud."
COCO CHANEL

"The power to question . . .
INDIRA GANDHI

. . . is the basis of all human progress."
INDIRA GANDHI

"With a new day . . .
ELEANOR ROOSEVELT

. . . comes new strength and new thoughts."
ELEANOR ROOSEVELT

Silent Quotes

Responsive Classroom®

Silent Quotes

Responsive Classroom®

Silent Quotes

Responsive Classroom®

Silent Quotes

Responsive Classroom®

Silent Quotes

Responsive Classroom®

Silent Quotes

Responsive Classroom®

Silent Quotes

Responsive Classroom®

Silent Quotes

Responsive Classroom®

Silent Quotes

Responsive Classroom®

Silent Quotes

Responsive Classroom®

Silent Quotes

Responsive Classroom®

Silent Quotes

Responsive Classroom®

Silent Quotes

Responsive Classroom®

Silent Quotes

Responsive Classroom®

Silent Quotes

Responsive Classroom®

Silent Quotes

Responsive Classroom®

"Action is . . .

JOAN BAEZ

. . . the antidote to despair."

JOAN BAEZ

"If you want to lift yourself up . . .

BOOKER T. WASHINGTON

. . . lift up someone else."

BOOKER T. WASHINGTON

"Amazing the things you find . . .

SACAGAWEA

. . . when you bother to
search for them."

SACAGAWEA

"Be brave. Take risks . . .

PAULO COELHO

. . . nothing can substitute
experience."

PAULO COELHO

"You are never strong enough . . .

CESAR CHAVEZ

. . . that you don't need help."

CESAR CHAVEZ

"The human mind is . . .

JOHN F. KENNEDY

. . . our fundamental resource."

JOHN F. KENNEDY

"We are never happy until . . .

DOROTHY DIX

. . . we learn to laugh
at ourselves."

DOROTHY DIX

"I never ran my train
off the track . . .

HARRIET TUBMAN

. . . and I never lost a passenger."

HARRIET TUBMAN

Silent Quotes

Responsive Classroom®

Silent Quotes

Responsive Classroom®

Silent Quotes

Responsive Classroom®

Silent Quotes

Responsive Classroom®

Silent Quotes

Responsive Classroom®

Silent Quotes

Responsive Classroom®

Silent Quotes

Responsive Classroom®

Silent Quotes

Responsive Classroom®

Silent Quotes

Responsive Classroom®

Silent Quotes

Responsive Classroom®

Silent Quotes

Responsive Classroom®

Silent Quotes

Responsive Classroom®

Silent Quotes

Responsive Classroom®

Silent Quotes

Responsive Classroom®

Silent Quotes

Responsive Classroom®

Silent Quotes

Responsive Classroom®

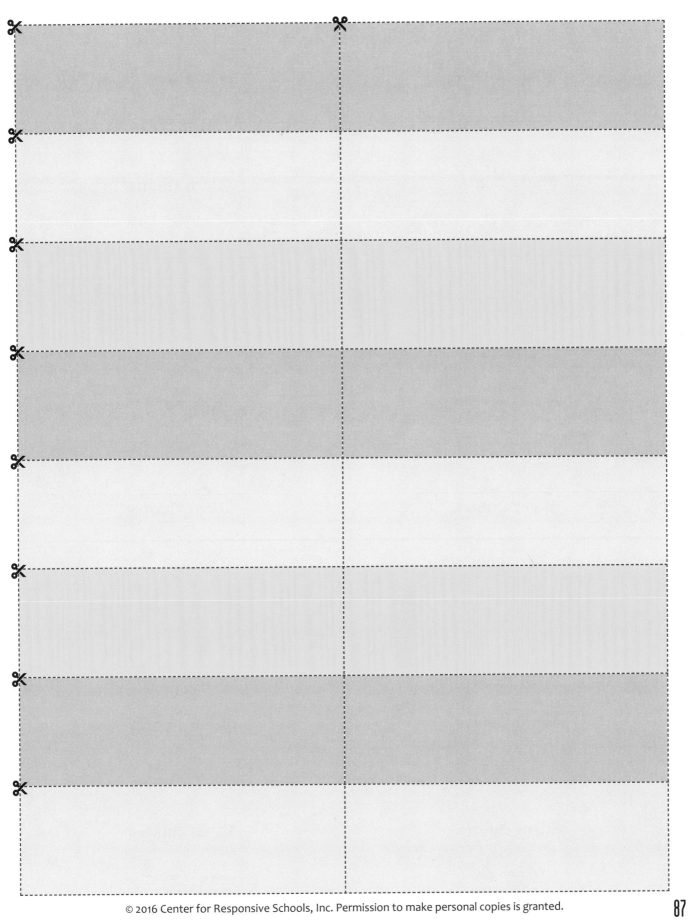

Silent Quotes

Silent Quotes

Responsive Classroom®

Silent Quotes

Responsive Classroom®

Silent Quotes

Responsive Classroom®

Silent Quotes

Responsive Classroom®

Silent Quotes

Responsive Classroom®

Silent Quotes

Responsive Classroom®

Silent Quotes

Responsive Classroom®

Silent Quotes

Responsive Classroom®

Silent Quotes

Responsive Classroom®

Silent Quotes

Responsive Classroom®

Silent Quotes

Responsive Classroom®

Silent Quotes

Responsive Classroom®

Silent Quotes

Responsive Classroom®

Silent Quotes

Responsive Classroom®

Silent Quotes

Responsive Classroom®

Silent Quotes

Responsive Classroom®

Brain Breaks Planner

	Monday	Tuesday	Wednesday	Thursday	Friday
Period:					
Period:					
Period:					
Period:					
Period:					
Period:					

Brain Breaks Planner

	Monday	Tuesday	Wednesday	Thursday	Friday
Period:					
Period:					
Period:					
Period:					
Period:					
Period:					

Further Resources

All the practices recommended in this book come from or are consistent with the *Responsive Classroom®* approach to teaching—an evidence-based education approach associated with greater teacher effectiveness, higher student achievement, and improved school climate. *Responsive Classroom* practices help educators build competencies in four interrelated domains: engaging academics, positive community, effective management, and developmentally responsive teaching. To learn more, see the following resources published by Center for Responsive Schools and available at www.responsiveclassroom.org.

Building an Academic Community: The Middle School Teacher's Guide to the First Four Weeks of the School Year (from *Responsive Classroom*, 2018). Bring order and organization to the first month of school while maintaining the enthusiasm and curiosity students bring with them as they start new routines and look ahead to a year's worth of learning.

Middle School Motivators: 22 Interactive Learning Structures (from *Responsive Classroom*, 2016). These easy-to-use structures encourage all students to give their best effort, focus on learning goals, and collaborate effectively with one another in dynamic, purposeful, and respectful ways.

The Power of Our Words for Middle School: Teacher Language That Helps Students Learn (from *Responsive Classroom*, 2016). Practical information, tips, and examples for improving the professional language you use with students. Through your use of words and tone, you can more fully engage students in their learning and support positive development in all areas of their lives.

The Responsive Advisory Meeting Book: 150+ Purposeful Plans for Middle School (from *Responsive Classroom*, 2018). Use the combination of structure, purpose, and planning in this book to strengthen and enrich your Advisory meetings, providing students with a safe place to build respectful, trusting relationships with peers and adults, explore their interests, and develop new skills.

Seeing the Good in Students: A Guide to Classroom Discipline in Middle School (from *Responsive Classroom*, 2019). Learn how to tap into young adolescents' desire for autonomy in order to help them become self-motivated to behave in productive and positive ways—to benefit themselves, their peers, and the greater school community.

Yardsticks: Child and Adolescent Development Ages 4–14, 4th ed. (by Chip Wood, 2017). This accessible reference concisely charts children's development, shows what behavior you can expect to see in the classroom (and at home) at different ages, and outlines ways you can support students' social-emotional and academic learning and growth.

Yardsticks Guide Series: Common Developmental Characteristics in the Classroom and at Home, Grades K–8 (from *Responsive Classroom*, 2018; based on *Yardsticks* by Chip Wood). Common characteristics of children's development are summarized in easy-to-scan, grade-specific guides for educators and parents.

ABOUT THE PUBLISHER

Center for Responsive Schools, Inc., a not-for-profit educational organization, is the developer of *Responsive Classroom®*, an evidence-based education approach associated with greater teacher effectiveness, higher student achievement, and improved school climate. *Responsive Classroom* practices help educators build competencies in four interrelated domains: engaging academics, positive community, effective management, and developmentally responsive teaching. We offer the following resources for educators:

PROFESSIONAL DEVELOPMENT SERVICES

- ➤ Workshops for K–8 educators (locations around the country and internationally)
- ➤ On-site consulting services to support implementation
- ➤ Resources for site-based study
- ➤ National conferences for K–8 educators

PUBLICATIONS AND RESOURCES

- ➤ Books on a wide variety of *Responsive Classroom* topics
- ➤ Free monthly newsletter
- ➤ Extensive library of free articles on our website

FOR DETAILS, CONTACT:

Responsive Classroom®

Center for Responsive Schools, Inc.
85 Avenue A, P.O. Box 718
Turners Falls, Massachusetts 01376-0718

800-360-6332 • www.responsiveclassroom.org
info@responsiveclassroom.org